LYDIA GRIGORIEVA

Shards from the Polar Ice

SELECTED POEMS

Translated by John Farndon with Olga Nakston

ИНСТИТУТ ПЕРЕВОДА

AD VERBUM

Published with the support
of the Institute for Literary Translation, Russia

GLAGOSLAV PUBLICATIONS

Shards from the Polar Ice
Selected Poems

by Lydia Grigorieva

Translated by John Farndon with Olga Nakston

Publishers Maxim Hodak & Max Mendor

Published with the support
of the Institute for Literary Translation, Russia

© 2015, Lydia Grigorieva

© 2016, Glagoslav Publications, United Kingdom

Glagoslav Publications Ltd
88-90 Hatton Garden
EC1N 8PN London
United Kingdom

www.glagoslav.com

ISBN: 978-1-78437-977-3

This book is in copyright. No part of this publication may be reproduced, stored in a retrieval system or transmitted in any form or by any means without the prior permission in writing of the publisher, nor be otherwise circulated in any form of binding or cover other than that in which it is published without a similar condition, including this condition, being imposed on the subsequent purchaser.

Introduction

I first came across Lydia Grigorieva's poetry in 2012 when I was working on a translation of her late husband Ravil Bukharaev's beautiful novel memoir *Letters to Another Room*. Ravil was a great poet himself, and it was quite clear from the book that he adored Lydia's poetry, too. He includes four full poems of hers within the text of the book and, of course, I had to translate these into English, so I came to see the power of her poetry at first hand.

One of the poems in particular stood out. It's called *Pity Beethoven* and is a short but highly charged tour de force that captures the romantic image of the genius raging against the world with tremendous power and theatricality. It's a piece that when read aloud to an audience thrills with its image of Beethoven striding through a storm. It makes poetry exciting, which is a rare quality.

"Cold rain rams his massive brow.
Balls of lightning hunt him now.
Sharp whips of wind about him lay.
Fate drives him on; he must obey."

The short, sharp, strongly rhythmic lines and vivid imagery are typical of Lydia's work, as I came to discover.

The poem was inspired, like so many of Lydia's poems, by an image she has seen on her travels around the world and responded to with characteristic intensity. Karlovy-Vary in the Czech republic was once known as Carlsbad. In the early 1800s, this elegant spa town in a deep wooded Bohemian cleft was the place to be, and Beethoven was just one of the famous visitors. Goethe, Chopin, Turgenev and many others came here to take the waters.

On the outskirts of the town there is a dynamic, wild looking statue of Beethoven, green with verdi-gris, his face turned as if in defiance of all that nature and the ages can throw at him. Inspired by the statue, Lydia creates an imaginary picture of the night when Beethoven walked through a storm here in the town to meet his 'Immortal Beloved' – and she creates it so vividly it's like a painting by Caspar David Friedrich come to life. And one can almost hear the crashing and defiant and desperate chords of Beethoven's music.

With that poem, I was intrigued, and then Lydia asked me to translate another of her poems, *A Dream in the Garden* – and I was hooked. The contrast with the Beethoven poem could not be starker. *A Dream in the Garden* is an intense, almost psychedelic vision of sensual love as a dream in a perfumed garden. It is utterly intoxicating with its flowers that drown the drunken young lovers with their heady scent. It's excessive, yes, but that's its power.

> *"And on your damp chest, it's not moths that are quivering*
> *But soft blushing petals, fallen and shivering."*

Whoever thought fallen petals could be so erotic?

I gradually learned of the high esteem which with Lydia's poems are held in Russia. Her poetry collections have been awarded numerous prizes. Her book of poems *Celestial* was shortlisted for the Buninskaya Prize and her *Eternal Theme* was finalist for Russian 'Book of the Year' in 2013. She won the Special Prize from the Russian Writers' Union (2010) for the best poetry book of the year for the collection featuring *A Dream in the Garden* and also the im. A. Delviga Prize (2012).

"It would be hard to imagine Russian poetry in the last half century without Lydia Grigorieva," writes eminent Russian poet and critic Konstantin Kedrov. But she is by no means an avant garde poet. Her poems are firmly traditional in their use of familiar rhythms and rhyme schemes. But that is her strength. Grigorieva is a uniquely individual voice, bucking trends of modernist poetry to create her own distinctive and beguiling body of poetry.

Her work draws on her own nomadic life to create arresting images and metaphors, full of beauty and power, vivid and arresting – whether it is white owls lost in the polar snow (*Arctic Ocean*) or tropic winds blowing through the pink palace of Jaipur (*The Palace of Winds*)

Sometimes her poems have the direct simplicity of a nursery rhyme or a traditional ballad.

"I'll sew a garden neatly
Stitch flowers in the waste
And the pollen floating sweetly
Will add a homely taste."

Sometimes the images are familiar:

"A white horse slowly, slowly trudging
Frail as mica, weakly panting
Enveloped by the winter steam."

Just as often they are enigmatic:

"And my green dog has lost its mind..."

But the imagery is always intriguing, often haunting.

Like the towering figure of Russian poetry, Alexander Pushkin, Lydia draws inspiration from the English romantics Byron and Coleridge. What is remarkable is how she uses these influences to tap deep into the heart of the terrible Russian experience under the Soviet Union, and the ravages wrought upon her beloved Ukraine, the place of her birth and an idyllic childhood.

In her haunting poem, *The Crazy Gardener*, the allusion to Coleridge's *Rhyme of the Ancient Mariner* is unmistakable:

"All the day long, the crazy old gardener
Worked on erecting an arbour of rose.
But the next day, as he walked out to water it,
Fear seized his soul and he instantly froze."

Yet this poem is a powerful image of the damage to the Russian soul of Communism – a soul endangered just as powerfully as Coleridge's mariner.

"There he was in the garden, candle in hand
Aglow in the day, with the sun shining bright
Illuminating the illogical landscape of Russia
And casting light on its dark soul's blight."

In the poem *Byron in Venice,* Pushkin and Byron actually both appear. They are linked in exile, and exile is a recurrent theme in Lydia's work, as it is in her life. Right now she lives in London as she has for decades since she came with her husband Ravil as he took up a job with the BBC World Service. It is the longest she has lived anywhere, but she is in exile from her homeland, from Russian Ukraine, the place of her birth, and the pain of those separations throbs like a vein through her poetry.

More than half her life, she spent under the Soviet regime, and like many poets came up against the constraints of the KGB, who, for instance, forbade any reference to God in poems. It's no wonder Russian poets became adept at speaking in riddles, and there are times when I am sure I have missed allusions when translating Lydia's poetry.

Lydia was born next to a cherry orchard in rural Ukraine. But when she was little more than a year old, the family moved to the Arctic, and it proved to be one of the shaping influences of her life and her poetry – and inspired not only the title of this collection, *Shards from the Polar Ice*, but a whole series of later poems. Her father, a polar reconnaissance pilot, died when his plane crashed in flames on an ice floe, and the tragedy has haunted her ever since.

But that infant time in the fantastic polar landscape, with its vast white expanses and its intense starlit nights, along with the horrific image of the burning plane far out on the ice inspired unforgettable poems, images often remembered through childish eyes.

"I wanted to turn the sky over,
Like a little handmade rug,
To see where the stars hide,"

Or:

*"And the blizzard came down,
Curling up like a husky –
You could tickle her behind her ear,"*

Her garden in London, carefully created over many years and providing a rich ground for her photopoetry, is another recurring theme, and her relationship with it has the intensity of a love affair, or a mother for a child.

*"My garden, my garden, my lush vineyard scene
My little boy innocent, little boy green."*

Lydia's poetry is full of such metaphors. Some are overt such as 'Cedar is my brother. The grass is my sister' that sounds almost like tribal animism. Some are more covert. But it is the richness of imagery, along with its musicality, that makes her poetry so captivating.

In this volume, there are just 80 of her poems, just a small portion of her life's work. We thought for a while that we should organize them chronologically, or geographically, but in the end we decided to arrange them randomly, so that each one provides a new surprise as you read through, with only a few grouped together, such as some of the Arctic poems.

Welcome to the poetic world of Lydia Grigorieva!

John Farndon
7th July 2016, London

A note on the Translation

Translating poems from another language is always a challenge, but Lydia's is particularly difficulty because of the centrality of rhyme and rhythm to her work. She believes the musicality of the verse is absolutely central to the poetic experience. So in creating these English versions, I knew I had to match her original step for step. Every translation has to follow the same rhyme scheme and meter precisely. No straight literal translation would ever do justice to her poems.

To make it harder, the different stress patterns of Russian words, and different rhyme possibilities, make it hard to replicate in English, without falling into the trap of losing the precision of meaning. Fortunately, I've been ably assisted by the superb literal translations provided for me by Olga Nakston, and of course by Lydia herself, who I am happy to report believes the translations are faithful to the originals.

John Farndon

Commentary by Konstantin Kedrov

It would be hard to imagine Russian poetry in the last half century without Lydia Grigorieva. Her lyrical voice of truth, recognizable and completely her own, is like no one else. Her creative biography merges with the geography of the Russian mainland. From the Arctic Ocean to the Donets Basin, and from there to Moscow and Kazan. In Kazan, where she was a student in her creative youth, she developed existential poetry, where a person, alone in the wide world, lies, covered with metaphor. From time to time, a shiver of poignant memories of her idyllic Ukrainian childhood merges with the immense sorrow for the ravaged country. Like every true poet Lydia Grigorieva is one in the world. Like every true poet, she belongs to the whole world. In London, she cultivates a vivid garden for her poetry, which in spite of all the time seems to grow younger and younger. Her poetry, like her garden, is full of vivid colours. Fragrant, aromatic, spicy. Then, too, there is the view from her window on the Arctic Ocean in the house ventilated by all the world's winds. Not adhering to any movements and currents, Lydia Grigorieva gives the world her delicate, vulnerable, smart lyrics. Smart as a mental prayer - for all, but only their own. She creatively takes off, and the trajectory of her poetic flight is into the infinite.

Konstantin Kedrov is an eminent Russian poet and critic, and winner of the 2013 Manhae prize for his book *Computer Love*.

Lydia Grigorieva

Shards from the Polar Ice
Selected Poems

Pity Beethoven

Pity Beethoven[1] – as he, grim-faced,
Through the vile and dark night raced.
Heedless of the waters' roar,
Through Carlsbad's sleeping streets he tore.

His speech was slurred and not quite sane.
He sped on through the gloom. In vane,
He clutched the air and clenched his fist
To crush to nought the damp night mist.

The awful storm brooks no escape.
The lightning twists into the shape
Of a vast tornado's maw –
No mortal can pass through this war.

Cold rain rams his massive brow.
Balls of lightning hunt him now.
Sharp whips of wind about him lay.
Fate drives him on; he must obey.

His green frock-coat is soaking wet.
But he cannot hear it yet!

---

1 This poem is inspired by the wild-looking bronze statue of the composer, now green with verdi-gris, that stands in a narrow ravine in Karlovy-Vary in the Czech Republic, formerly Carlsbad. It commemorates the night when Beethoven set off through a storm here to meet his 'immortal beloved' – and perfectly captures the image of the heroic romantic genius defying nature.

LYDIA GRIGORIEVA

The crash, the floods, land going under...
And then the booming claps of thunder.

Oh yes, wake up, and clap the sight:
Beethoven striding through the night!

A Dream in the Garden

Oh yes, I will tell you – and I know you will me hear me –
Of a dream in the garden beneath the old pear tree
Beneath the white apple in light gold and hazy,
Beneath the blue lilac, the air sweet and lazy.

In the bright moonlit garden, in honeyed grass sunken
You in my dream – young, moody and drunken
With unquenchable passion, and love fierce and true,
Beneath hoarfrosted cherries, plums wet with dew.

There in my dream, it's all so much clearer:
The almond bloom's gone, apricot's time is nearer
And on your damp chest, it's not moths that are quivering
But soft blushing petals, fallen and shivering.

Every leaf, every bloom, exhales fragrance so forcefully
That to dream of the garden is no longer enough for me
I long to wake up, with you at my side;
I must catch and hold on to that illusory tide.

And bright breeze-blown blossom whirls pink in the air
As we love in reality and you are right there
As the petals of love heavenwards stream
And once more I dream of a dream of a dream...

LYDIA GRIGORIEVA

The Polar Day[2]

I wanted to turn the sky over,
Like a little handmade rug,
To see where the stars hide,
Where, like clusters of celestial forgen-me-nots
Studding dense tundra grass,
They adorn the vault of heaven...
I was about five years old...
Like a tiny kitten, I was learning to see,
Gazing wide-eyed at the world around –
Still free to wish the impossible...
The weeping Virgin bent low from the skies...
My young and lovely mother
Waiting for father, laughing, singing,
Walking through the tundra to gather stars...
She had other things to think about:
To love me,
To shake out the handmade rug,
Not to shake the stars...
And that starry sky was lying in our home
Within reach.

While father flew over the ocean
Embroidered with sky-blue ice,
Those blue forget-me-not clusters

---

2   Lydia Grigorieva lived for some years during her early childhood in the very north of Russia, in the Arctic circle, where her young father flew reconnaissance missions out over the Arctic Ocean. He was killed when his plane crashed on the ice, and the tragic event inspired many of Lydia Grigorieva's later poems. After the crash, little Lydia and her mother returned to Ukraine.

Climbed the vault of heaven
Through the polar day
To shine in the gaping void...
Father knew how to find his way home from the stars...
And mother knew how to wait...

LYDIA GRIGORIEVA

The Polac Night

1.
And the blizzard came down,
Curling up like a husky –
You could tickle her behind her ear,
But I was scared – this word
Struck terror in my childish soul:
I could hear through the clay walls
How she howled and ripped to shreds
The vastness. And so
Those icy shards of polar night flew
And rapped against our windows.
And in the morning this little wooden house
In this Arctic village will be buried up
To its chimney.
We will not be found: while father is flying far off
Over distant floes,
No-one will miss mother and me...

Then he will come flying,
Will land – so tall and jolly,
Smelling of icy interstellar wind,
Smelling of chilly iridescent petrol:
Himself – golden with vitality,
Himself – lit up by the glow
Of our shining, happy faces...

He used to take me for walks – not along the boulevard
But by the Arctic Ocean...

And the sky was covered with icy shards
Of never fading polar stars. I don't remember it

Starless in the far far North:
It was always blazing and aglow,
Shining and shooting
And swirling into a funnel... into the abyss.

And it is still so – the cosmic bonfire
Of the Northern Lights shines but gives no warmth,
Flickering through the density of time, lighting
The bumpy sledge path of my fate...

2.
I didn't decide my fate,
This accident decided me...
Father in his burning plane
Didn't think about himself –
But of me:
And so I grew sheltered and warm –
The plane crashed with him
And heated a huge space...

3.
This is my life, father – a frail vessel
Given substance by another!
We will meet on the transcendent flight
Over the endless fields of ice.

4.
I put my hands in the Yenisei
They froze and then relaxed.
Now all my life will not be enough
To find my father's grave.

LYDIA GRIGORIEVA

* * *

A life among the stones I took
Like the lizard and the lichen clump
Like moss, I crept through every nook,
Clung tight to every rocky hump.

I wound myself on branch and bough,
Like vine, the trees became my lair
To conquer every inch somehow
Under vasty seas of air.

The Crazy Gardener

All the day long, the crazy old gardener
Tended his flowers and planted his seeds
But the next day, his labours had vanished
And the overgrown beds were strangled by weeds.

All the day long, the crazy old gardener
Worked on erecting an arbour of rose
But the next day as he walked out to water it
Fear seized his soul and he instantly froze.

All the day long, he bent his old back
Heaving the arches once more in a row
And the next day, he went out to see
His work all in ruins, blooms buried below.

And was the old gardener crazy or sane
As he surveyed the wreckage with candle in hand?
Where was the deity amidst the ruins?
This was a world he could not understand.

There he was in the garden, candle in hand
Aglow in the day, with the sun shining bright
Illuminating the illogical landscape of Russia
And casting light on its dark soul's blight.

LYDIA GRIGORIEVA

* * *

R.B.[3]

How we danced then, you and I,
In the piazza, one chill Venice night!
The Moon whirling on through the lustrous sky –
A star held in its soft, crescent light.

Not in vane – it seemed back then –
To break off from life in mid-phrase,
And venture out on the seas again
With our sorrow and the love of days.

A thread of melodies slowly unwound
And the jazz kicked the heart with its beat
And the carnival crowd thronging thickly around
Saw sense and made space for our feet.

In such truly magical places and instants
It's not hard to forget years passed by
And fly far from the stifling present
Under heaven's all-watchful eye.

This way and that, we whirled 'cross the floor
Beneath that celestial gaze,
And soon attuned to the rhythm once more
Of that time, and the whole world and its days.

And the infinite skies shimmered and shone
In the dark Venice waters there
And we that night again came upon
Both youth's spring and boundless despair.

---

[3] Ravil Bukharaev, Lydia's late husband.

Vivaldi in Venice

Here, in Venice, at the very beginning –
Where the vagrant moon raises its light,
Where the swell sets the gondolas rocking,
Where each night Vivaldi lies sighing –
I shrug as I'm standing there wondering:
Why such a bitter cold night?

Here, where the waves are slip-slapping,
Plucking mud from the sea in the bight,
Where masonry's gradually crumbling –
There Vivaldi is sighing and yearning
To know what the future will bring him:
Why such a bitter cold night?

And like a mirage, look, there it's floating –
Someone's face in the vapourous light,
Deceiving us and seducing
Our souls to start tenderly singing –
Here, Vivaldi sighed, little fretting:
Why such a bitter cold night?

LYDIA GRIGORIEVA

Cedar is my brother. The grass is my sister...
R. Bukharaev[4]

My brother's a stag – my sister an owl, too;
I love each as their status is due.
I love each of my kith according to kind –
For silver, for gold, for gifts of the mind.

And I will aver before I begin:
The slippery ide and chir[5] are my kin.
And I insist that my family must be
Grey seals and leopard seals, lions of the sea.

I was raised between water and sky –
This is a truth that I cannot deny.
The whiskery walrus, the great polar bear
Were my truest ancestors, I have to declare.

Beneath the bird's cry – far out from the shore –
When the polar plane downed on the ice long before.
But my father is laughing, with eagle-like eyes.
That's how I live: beneath wing, beneath skies.

---

4   The late Ravil Bukharaev (1951-2012) was Lydia Grigorieva's husband. A Russian Tatar and an Ahmaddiya muslim, Ravil Bukharaev was a celebrated poet and historian himself. His beautiful, poetic memoir of his life with Lydia has been translated as 'Letters to Another Room' by John Farndon with Olga Nakston (Renaissance, 2014).

5   The ide and chir are river fish of the northern Siberian rivers.

Wet...

Wallops of wind in drunken desperation
Beating their heads against the paving
Then suddenly, viciously – a knife to the heart
Brrrmm!
So softly and so evenly
Pressing upon the flesh of the brain
Fear, spurting like a severed vein
Fear, as I dive in into an alley,
Then glance back...
Lanky, one-legged, a pursuing torch
Its beam askew
Randomly flashing
I squeeze up to let him bend and shiver,
And tuck into my shelter
"Off with the light, you one-legged beanstalk!"
I bark abruptly
And the torch goes dark at once
BRRMMM...louder.
I peer into the street and see
Searchlights sweeping to and fro
Blindly flashing, lonely eyes,
Remorselessly catching puddles, blinking pools
As they try to steady.
BRRMMM!!... ever louder.
Light swelling, beams closing in
BRRRRRMMMMM!!...deafening!
...Then wind and rain, wind, rain
And the plane climbing away...

LYDIA GRIGORIEVA

* * *

Will it be our children
who snap the last branch off the tree of life?
Will it be our grandchildren
                        who crush the last forget-me-not
to dust beneath their feet and don't even notice?
Even Angels fight to breathe
                        beneath the wheezing ozone
over the rubbery ices of Antarctica!
As if we're getting even
with that power of the universe
that created us:
Well – now we're even.

* * *

These are difficult times at best –
Of vacuous, vapid lies.
To live is like building a chimney breast
With bricks of different size.

It should be deeply engraved on the brow
To remind the young what they lack.
My life's been entirely sucked out of me now
Like smoke up the chimney stack.

LYDIA GRIGORIEVA

In the Garden of a Communist

In the garden of a communist, it is ever cold and dead
And all around there rings a hollow nothingness.
In the garden of a democrat, it's a lush, warm flowerbed
But beyond it stretches the pauper's emptiness.

Through a chill backstreet I stumble,
                               as the ice begins to harden
A brother's what I need – God, why not give me that?
There's ample room for all in
                               the communist's great garden
And even more on offer in the garden of a democrat.

* * *

I'll suit my life, I'll make it trim
I'll tailor it once more
A house upon the woodland's rim
Stretching out beyond the door.

I'll sew a garden neatly
Stitch flowers in the waste
And the pollen floating sweetly
Will add a homely taste.

It's not easy finding comfort's way
In these forgetful rooms...
When your home is far away
From your family tombs.

5.11.09

LYDIA GRIGORIEVA

* * *

I flung the door wide
But there's no-one to see...
Hold dear, you beasts outside,
My dear son for me...

I'll share the water freely
From the deep well in the green
Is it such a sin for me
To grieve on and to keen?

I'll drink water from the pond.
I'll stray out in the woods.
Hold dear, you birds beyond,
My dear son in the clouds...

08.11.2009

White Horse[6]

White horse – lean and lofty!
Close along the roadside quietly
Right next to the ice's rim,
A white horse slowly, slowly trudging
Frail as mica, weakly panting
Enveloped by the winter steam.

A wintry waste, dark and chilly...
Now the night is falling swiftly
From the canal across the way.
The heroic horse – lean and lofty
Bearing its heavy load so staunchly!
White! White as a winter's day.

---

6   In the Russian original, the word for white is *bled* (pale) and has a strong association with one of the four horses of the Apocalypse, the white horse of conquest and pestilence, but also victory.

LYDIA GRIGORIEVA

* * *

My garden, my garden, my lush vineyard scene
My little boy innocent, little boy green.

You sweep clean away the pitch dark of night
My meek little one, my humble young wight.

I will never forget to the end of my days
How I prayed for this miracle, oh how I prayed.

How I cherished and raised you so tenderly
But then in the end I released you from me.

And how I left you one day for a bride
Beyond heaven's garden, a-wandering wide.

16 August 1999

Verde que te queiro verde...[7]
F.G. Lorca

Here was another phrase, a lacerating wound.
Twenty four times – the revolver's shattering sound.

Scorching the palate with blazing verbal kisses
Twenty four skies and twenty four abysses.

The truth out in an open field matches sorrow's burn:
Twenty four agonies; twenty four screams in turn.

You blindly obeyed the hollow words they said:
Blue like the sky or, like an abyss, red.

Ears filled with soft words – blown with evil seeds before:
Reeking of bovine spirit, stenched by lion's maw.

A phrase caught by the torn dragnet of the past
Twenty four times – each one the last.

---

[7] 'Green, I want you green.' From Frederico Garcia Lorca's poem. The Spanish poet Lorca (1898-1936) was taken out into the forest and shot by a group of fascist Nationalist militia in 1938 at the beginning of the Spanish Civil War.

LYDIA GRIGORIEVA

* * *

Smash the window and throw yourself out!
There's life! There's night!
Trees are bent...
Smashed into blood,
Weeping and crying,
But never sleep or fall idle.

And stick wrapping paper to your face
To absorb the cold sweat
Or lie in calm and darkness
Until the pain passes away...

Or you can try this: hang on a branch upside down
And create a poem...
And everything else, I can hand around
Like slices of bread...

But no-one will take them...
Or you can unlock the reason for these unreasonable tears
And dry them up.
All would be possible were it not for the whir
And screech of the passing cars.

18.10.1967
Kazan

Shostakovich

The Fifth Symphony[8]

Under his breath, he spoke to the century.
He beat the drums full and played the pipes loudly.
In his music, he turned turmoil and sorrow
Into a storm beneath the violin bow –
The piano pedal pressed down hard and clear,
So it could never scream out in fear.

Throwing on his coat in a thoughtful adagio,
He drove his way home through the falling snow,
And lay down in the dark in the marital bed.
But the wild blizzard buzzed inside his head,
And a vast wilderness yawned away
Beneath the dense mass of the camel duvet.

He lay like that until Venus rose high
And all of a sudden music started to fly,
After incubating inside through the night
Though his vision was blurred, he had found his insight –
Either the orchestral opening was racing away
Or the ceiling crashed down like a great bird of prey.

How to let go, release the harmony,
When the sound still sat inside him silently,
He has not been able to find a way.

---

8   The premier of Shostakovich's Fifth took place in 1937 at the height of Stalin's repressions and the composer was under intense scrutiny after the outrage at the artiness of his Lady Macbeth of Mtensk.

LYDIA GRIGORIEVA

Yet Time swoops down like that big bird of prey,
Clawing chords down in front of everybody.
An outburst of cheers. A wild victory...

Rose Petals

If I weave a life from rose petals –
They will wither.
If I sew a dress from rose petals –
They'll be crushed.
If I eat a rose petal –
It will dissolve in my mouth.
If I cover myself with rose petals –
I will freeze
Strew my grave with rose petals –
I will rise.

In the gloomy attic where webs hang low
A dead artist paints, hand moving slow.

A diagonal. A line to the right.
A yellow streak here. The temple – white.

And before him perched on a fold-up chair
A nude girl with red beret on long blonde hair.

A line to the left. Two lines coalesce.
There'll be a picture. There'll be a success.

The painting's gone on an age and a day:
Family, children and neighbours have long passed away.

The dead hand glides, watched by a dead eye:
Only the foolish will curl up and die.

A pale white body. A curving line here.
A dusky blue hue. A jagged red smear.

The artist has died. He struggles to stand.
His distant descendants will admire his hand.

A feast of lines. That shoulder – so pale
Strength and genius. This picture's for sale.

24.04.67
Kazan

Arctic Ocean

Let us fly, my dear soul, let us fly
Through blizzards of white, you and I!
We'll surf on the tail of the storm at its height
On through the black of the long polar night!

Like this paper, and the words that I write,
Black eyes of an owl white as white
Stare out in surprise from drifts of deep snow –
Ah well, here it's always been so.

We flew off where the land falls away
Where the white fox's tracks fast decay
Where the far northern lights
                        drape their hues through the night.
Where my soul is weighed in the balance each night.

This is where, in my lost infanthood,
My father in reindeer boots stood
By the fragile fuselage with his hand on his hip
Before soaring away, on his last earthly trip.

Over and over, I see in my dreams:
We fly on, wing blazing, it always seems.
Fly on, dear soul, fly – fly far and away.
We've flown on and on since that fateful day.

Black cinders on white icy shards...
But we still need alphabet cards
For these symbols of life through the years
In this place where snow buries your tears.

LYDIA GRIGORIEVA

And where I speed on in despair
A single wing raking the air,
Where in icy oblivion around the north pole
Rolls the chill Arctic Ocean of my poor soul.

Arctic Circle

Once memories are fleshed out with words,
Like a ticking bomb they resonate.
The snowy owl – whitest of birds:
To some a jewel, to me – it's fate.

The sled-weary reindeer treds this way:
Exotic to some, memories to me.
The bright and boisterous Arctic day:
Mum cries and faints – that's all I see.

The aircraft wing so clearly dud:
Well, it was sound not long ago.
The flames burst out. The sickening thud.
Hard to recall. To live with, more so.

The child dreams on the train in warmth:
We're going home to Ukraine here.
We roll, mum and I, with all the Earth.
I dream the owl. I freeze with fear.

At last, the Arctic Circle's whole;
Inside it, calm, I fall asleep.
That's where, pa, cold caught my soul.
That's where I glimpsed into the deep.

LYDIA GRIGORIEVA

Byron in Venice[9]

It is not without meaning that a poet's journey
Is lengthy and dangerous and filled with mystery.
So Byron goes to Venice and Pushkin to Crimea
Secretly, each alone, they slowly draw near.

The reins must be gripped, firm round the neck,
For the trot to stay steady and the power held in check.
To bring calm to the soul. See the world in peace.
To give back the land to the peasants in Greece.

From the Crimean steppes to the Odessian bay
Where dreams bring sharp tears and lovers betray.
Where come stanzas, ballads and orient lays
And lines sung for 'Onegin' when the wind plays.

The crown of Chrysostom is never so sweet
With unnumbered miles passed under your feet
And oarsmen are hampered by life's sea as they row.
How alike is the doom of a great bard, you must know?

The crystalline moon shines bright in the sky
But Byron in Venice has drunk it all dry.
His inkwell is empty. Europe's drowned now in sin.
And the tears of Augusta[10] are in glass, frozen in.

---

9   The poet Lord Byron *1788-1844) spent much of his life travelling through Europe and arrived in Venice in 1816. It was here that he wrote Childe Harold, and conducted various affairs with Venetian women, one of whom, the tempestuous Margarita Cogni, threw herself into a canal after a fight.

10   Augusta Leigh Byron (1783-1788), Byron's half-sister, who the

Oh poor Abyss!

Deep void beyond the sky, beyond our sight:
Oh poor Abyss! Is there no end to your dark night?

The Moon, out of the mist, unsheathed its blade.
Where can it, its raging grief displace
If there's no bottom, no bounds to empty space?

The storms of time uproot the oaken tree.
The Moon-slayer sees just infinity.

No pen stroke delineates the space.
The black hole stretches limitless away...
Not for nothing in this way does pitch dark hold sway.

Oh it's black in Rus[11] – it's time to save the saints!
Tendons tremble at the horror – someone faints.

"Come on, let's play hide and seek now, kids!
But where, when there is neither base nor lids?"

The Moon's shift rips and with the lashing rain
Fear comes down like some sly thug again.

---

poet is rumoured to have had an incestuous affair with. Byron may also have fathered Augusta's third daughter Elizabeth Medora the year before his Venice trip, which some say was made to escape prosecution for the relationship. 'Medora' is the name a heroine in Byron's poem 'The Corsair', written at Newstead Abbey when the poet and a pregnant Augusta were snowbound together in 1814. But Medora was brought up along with Augusta's other daughters unaware that Byron might be her father.

11   An old name for Russia.

LYDIA GRIGORIEVA

Don't look back now you've begun – just flash your
heels and run.

"Bare boards squeaking – where's a hiding place,
Where's the game end, when there's no end to space?
No cupboard, chest nor some concealing nook.
In all nature, darkness everywhere you look.
But some malicious hunger drives you on;
It whips you, and beats you on and on."

And in the boundless dark, beyond all sight –
Children cry 'Father' pitifully through the night.

The neglected Garden

Here's a soul's garden neglected and dank
without love without care a desolate blank
dense jasmine and lilac grow over the bank
raspberries and blackberries thorny and rank

if some bold stranger ventures inside
in the green shadows where lost truths now hide
crunching like ice underfoot with each stride
on leaves and blooms fallen in piles deep and wide

the anguish is neither implied nor intended
but it's magnified greatly by fear's chill and doubt
and I'm unsure what's broken can ever be mended:
if one entered here – would they ever get out?

LYDIA GRIGORIEVA

The Age of Silver[12]

In real life and dreams, all that ever came true
Was the chill breath of winter that always blew –
And the snow, the snow and the snow...

This Age of Silver sticks cold to the pane
And glistens both inside and outside again
In a poem, a poem, a poem...

Though we ripped into life with such reckless greed
We never begged once for alms nor for bread
With salt tears of blame - no, oh no.

For the lost and absurd who lived far too late,
The snow glitters bright on the wide plains of fate
Of their home, their home, their home.

The ages whirl by like the drifting of snows.
On the far white horizon, a brilliant line glows
Of Russian words that endure ever more.

The blizzard sweeps over us, heaping on snow
Avalanches of words, a thick verbal floe,
As before, before, as before...

---

12 The Silver Age is the name sometimes applied to a very creative period of Russian poetry, from the 1890s to the end of the civil war and corresponding to the Fin de siècle and Belle Époque. It is said to have been launched by Alexander Blok's poem 'Verses to the Beautiful Lady', and was driven by the Russian Symbolist and Futurist movements. Anna Akhmatova, Boris Pasternak and Osip Mandelstam all began writing at this time.

Kantemir[13] in London

The Empress sent you far away
To London – but what could you say?
I will walk down that same street
And I will remember when we meet.

I'll dawdle by the Thames so clear
In the footsteps of Antioch Kantemir.

Shadows flicker down each lane
And danger lurks in all the nooks
Our bard wasn't a boozer nor insane –
But that's no help when you deal with crooks

Kantemir liked music and he liked art
And everything that's wise and witty
But beer in the glass foams like a fart
And it's oh so noisy in this seedy city.

He came on foot here to this din
But in foreign lands, even air's a sin.

And when his heart fell in the snare
Of a courtesan of beauty rare,
The wise young man declined a tumble

---

13   Antiochus Kantemir (1708-1744) was a Moldavian diplomat in the Russian empire, sometimes described as 'the father of Russian poetry'. He was sent as ambassador to London aged 23 from 1731 to 1736, against his will, and then went to Paris, where he met Montesquieu and Voltaire, and died aged just 35. His most famous poem 'Petrida' is an unfinished epic that makes a hero of Peter the Great.

LYDIA GRIGORIEVA

With proud wrath his voice did rumble.

And In our hearts, the silent lyre
Plays for Antioch Kantemir....

And with a delirious sneeze and sigh
Young Kantemir did promptly fly.
In Paris, and down by the Seine
He vanished in thick mist and rain.

So the wraith of night was stayed
And as Trediakovsky[14] surely said:
"I'll end with a flute this mournful lay
Of Russians when they're away."

---

14   Vasily Trediakovsky (1703-1769), a Russian poet and contemporary of Kantemir.

* * *

Once more I had to, as long ago,
Conquer the blizzard entirely alone,
With Rus and lynx and elk in the snow
That buried them all up to the hip bone.

No-one looked after me, here, or cared;
There was no-one watching for me.
Inside, some small creature left me unspared
As it gnawed on my soul tirelessly.

An unheard of snowfall covered the way
To the home station I needed to reach.
But the creature inside showed no dismay,
Sucking the wounds like a leech.

And yet I gathered the strength to stand tall
To drive grief away from my heart.
To shake myself free from that deep, deep snowfall,
Tread it down and make the drifts part.

LYDIA GRIGORIEVA

Flight Analysis

In New York, you go down into the abyss
In a moment, you vanish into the mist
Lost in the crush of the Wall Street time
Buried in the depths of human slime.

Or if you go to Paris, say
Wafting coach plumes the boulevarde way...
But this is all just a fictional stew
Which you're directly heiress to.

Or to go back? Where? Oh my!
To live out my life on Filevskaya[15]
Where we've neither house nor fence before?
Our son is not with us any more!

If only, if only I'd died with grief!
Now I race over the Earth like a witch on a broom
Looking for a camp or sheltering room
As if I am some cunning thief.

And if I ride my broom through the air
In London's multicultural layer.

This is the place that fate's mould takes
And here I was born to Baikal's lake.
Under the wing of Ulan Bator
In a Ukrainian native khutor[16].

---

15 A street in Moscow where Lydia and her husband once lived with her late son.
16 A traditional Ukrainian homestead.

How did I end up in these heights here?
I should ask my mum, Marusya..

* * *

Words displayed upon the shelf enact
Pitchers, vases, amphorae of old.
They glisten in the sun, refract
And magnify one-hundredfold,

But words are brittler than crystal glass
More fragile too than porcelain
And so they're used fearfully and fast
And quickly put away again.

Much better hide them well away
Safe from harm where none will see –
In the dresser for another day
Firmly under lock and key.

Monument

Some might depart forever, and no trace will be found
Or mentioned then just fade away...
But I have a monument of flowers planted in the ground
That will neither wither or decay.

While people argue endlessly over entries to a book
Disputing over day or night,
A coloured stream glows in me – look –
And makes the darkness bright.

LYDIA GRIGORIEVA

Passion for Colours

Lilac pink purple aquamarine
Gold, turquoise, deep cobalt blue
Orange sienna emerald green
Crimson lavender too.

Apple apricot pale gooseberry
Blackcurrant lemon dark plum
Claret cerise crimson strawberry
Post Office red - as they come.

Summer sky blues fresh-mown grass green
Autumn leaf russet and umber
Battleship grey, bloody carmine
Cabbage red, violet and amber.

Silvery moon dusky brown hues
Emperor purple soft fawn
Dark evergreen lavender blues
Scarlet and ruby of dawn.

* * *

I'm stepping through anguish once more –
Pressure, numbness and despair –
To hang the washing out the backdoor
Beneath the peach blossom and the pear.

The softly fluttering flowers present
A balance to the strife and pain.
Your shirts absorb the healing scent
That lingers on beyond the rain.

The dense and confined gloom inside
Make thick oppressive clouds arise.
But the clothes are getting dried
In the garden under starry skies.

LYDIA GRIGORIEVA

Eternal Subjecte

"*A Muse doesn't worry about an income...*»
Korean poet Chan Zhon Il[17]

Here is the tower of Hölderlin[18]
On the banks of an insufficient river.

Here's a rotund tower on the riverbank
in an ancient Swabian town,
where centuries splash sleepily
and raise their brows over the eternal subject
of the poet's insanity, and fix their empty gaze
upon vacant words about the notion
that a Muse cares not about an income,
ever-focused on the eternal and so ensures
that the poet in his yellow home
on the banks of some dull Swabian river
lives locked up and walks in circles
for three decades, and gets followed
as if by faithful dogs
by global glory never fading,
by immortality, and by the horror
of everyday poverty...

02.12.07

---

17   Korean poet Chang Chinsong or Jang Jinseong who defected from North to South in 2005 and who lives under threat from the North Korean government.

18   A round yellow towerhouse in Tubingen, Germany, where the romantic poet Friedrich Hölderlin (1770-1843), declared insane, spent thirty years of his life in complete isolation.

* * *

All's long been wrong for me… I know it…
Why would I ever need this stolen world
This small house and this overcoat?

It's long seemed pointless… you see…
Why would I ever need this second-rate drama
And this ancient movie?

I live on credit, accidentally
Why would I ever need this nourishing broth
And this strong aromatic tea?

For sure, I blame the whole world now!
Why would I ever need this makeshift soul
And the deep sadness on my brow?

Poet and Muse

Henri Rousseau[19] lived in the woods
among flamboyant flower buds.
Half-tones were aliens in his world
and foliage, dense and lush,
shielded him from light
Greedy-green
and poisonous-scarlet
prevailed upon his canvases.
And his friend Guillaume Apollinaire[20]
appeared in the guise of a commoner
of an overage and cunning dunce.
He was a guest in an imaginary forest
and etched in my mind
in the picture I love so much.
Oh, a child's chill imagination!
Apollinaire has brought his dear one
into the forest to the "customs man"[21].
And here in the forest they –
on soft grasses,
among the dazzling flowers of Asia Minor –
stayed for a long time...
This must be why
they have such a ridiculous look

---

19   The French Post-Impressionist painter Henri Rousseau (1844-1910), known for his naïve jungle scenes, even though he only left Paris in his imagination.

20   French poet and playwright Guillaume Apollinaire (1880-1918), a pioneer of Surrealism, and a friend of Picasso as well as Rousseau.

21   A reference to Rousseau's nickname Le Douanier (the customs officer) – he worked as a toll collector.

like children who misbehaved.
Oh, this forest is the palace of his creations!
When I enter it,
my head spins
from the spicy fumes
and love.

1980

Dreaming

A dream – is a propeller blade,
the decayed silk
of a Chinese fan.
A dream – is an abyss,
in which it's sweet to fall.
A dream – is a scrap of fear
and a child's secret passion.

A dream – is a ginger clown,
a healing cavern,
a TB sanatorium
and sweet anguish on the face.

1986

* * *

The lilac by the home of Pasternak
Is blanketed with snow.
A sign we looked for sometime back –
An enigmatic show.

They used to live here nicely
But perhaps could've lived better
If only words and harmony
Were put upon the altar.

And past midnight in the silence
The earthly court ignored;
Hungering for the soul's ascendance
To the celestial heights they soared.

And the church upon the hillslope
Seemed entirely fit
For the rampant and uplifting scope
Of the home of honoured lit.

How did he live in all that time -
A hermit and recluse?
The empty house entombed in rime
The silence so diffuse.

But the light's still shining
Forgiven and forgiving
All the fates still favouring
His soul baptised and living.

LYDIA GRIGORIEVA

A textbook line can't be undone
With blasphemy and blackened name.
A memory is a touchstone
For everlasting national fame.

December 1987
Peredelkino

The Mad Photographer

Like a greedy bumblebee, a-buzzing and desiring,
I hover and peer fervently above the open bloom...

Such a keen eagerness and inquiring zeal
You've never seen before. Let's talk –
about exposure, focus and zoom...

What can be more beautiful and more insane
than a glowing, satin petal?

A bumblebee shoots past my brow
And look, I'm hovering, soaring now
Barefooted, sick and weightless – how?
Over the deep red throat of an open flower.

Yes, I'll sell it all, under the hammer it goes:
the passion, fragility and power,
the luscious pink, decked in feathers, and the nudity
of so young a creature, oh...

Of this molested beauty
Who bared all...

Look, look, a tulip party has
Thrown off all its clothes. What a nation
Nature is to unloose so many things!

A camera – is a mystical device!
And when nature's in profusion
and I enrapt with crazy passion

LYDIA GRIGORIEVA

pounce upon to these candy treats
which are called more plainly flowers.

But how similar they are to folk
with their bloom and bitter withering!...
And so I pay them tribute
Soaring in Paradise, day and night,
(zoom in closer, zoom), without ever falling...

22.05.04
London

* * *

I thank you now, my verdant wood.
As I walked between snout-features,
Your thick foliage understood
And hid me from these creatures.

I thank you now, my garden green,
For your roses' thorny wall,
Ensuring that I won't be seen
And my foes can't reach at all.

I thank you now, my husband dear,
For protecting me so well
Far up on the mountain's spear
All through that time of hell.

The century-old midnight hum:
A moot of trees, their majlis,
Spurred me on as I did come
To exist between the foxes.

And to be among the stars, Father,
Among birds, between moon and sun
I thank you now, dear Father
For the wet night just begun.

19.08.02

LYDIA GRIGORIEVA

* * *

Oh, how can we, can we be so daring?
Have we, have we lost our minds?
No, we don't want angels seeing –
I should quickly close the blinds!

And just in case it seems enticing,
I should shut the door at least
While we go on intertwining
Wildly, like two young beasts.

Why do I feel such misgiving
Slicing between us like a breeze?
As if some unseen wings are beating
Fretfully, in their unease.

Soon, you'll drift off into sleep, dear,
Reassured and tired for now.
But through the darkness, I'll stare on here:
That's why we stayed adjoined somehow.

And as our breaths slow by and by
And silence steals across the floor,
I pull the blinds and it's as if I
Frightened someone off once more.

05.10.04

*'God save me from losing my mind,
I'd rather walk off with a staff and a bag.'
Alexander Pushkin[22]*

And my green dog has lost its mind.
And my green dog has lost its mind.
And my green dog has lost its mind –
It makes me weep.

Is he off with his bag, poor and ill?
Is he off with his bag, poor and ill?
Is he off with his bag, poor and ill?
My sad green friend...

My sad green dog was a brother to me.
Don't stand by the gate, come back to me!
Or shall I come along with you –
Where is my staff?

---

22   The foremost Russian poet Alexander Pushkin (1799-1837). Pushkin died in a duel, aged just 38, the subject of a play of mine, 'The Naked Guest'.

LYDIA GRIGORIEVA

* * *

Oh God in your heaven, with purpose
                             and work fill my home
You can truly believe I will never deny you
Come fill my heart to the brim with love for you.

* * *

Michelangelo went to Carrara[23] to choose
a slab of marble
only he needed
and swept the piles of rubbish
from the Sistine Chapel
after the working day.

May your broom
at last have bristles
and become as silvery
as the sacred willow
in the Cathedral
on Karlovy-Vary's peak.
Take it quickly in your hands!
Sweep out the piles of rubbish
that litter
every corner
of your soul.

---

[23] The famous marble quarries in Tuscany used since the times of Ancient Rome and where Michelangelo got the stone for his most famous statues.

LYDIA GRIGORIEVA

Raising a Garden

The cast iron heavy day weighs down upon the earth
But my garden will not give goosefoot nor thistle berth.

My garden's not a brother nor is kin to any other
He expected to be raised –
                                      it was he who raised me rather.

He used to be quite naked but now he's fully dressed
A coat of rose-pink petals has lain over his chest.

In London's wilderness,
                           this rude youngster came to learn
An eclipse of the soul, the eclipse of hearts in turn.

With down-to-earth disdain, he burst upon the scene
But high-fashion attire has clothed his natural green.

With all the scented herbs
                                 and sun-flecked blossom laying
He's now quite civilized, his embroidery displaying.

And kinship is not fixed nor knows of any bound
I love him when I work him and kneel upon his ground.

10.08.99

An Angel Coming

Yes, it's been written – but maybe then forgotten
Or tainted with a lie.
Were they annointed, named or just appointed:
God's angels on high?

Why were those presentations subject to alterations -
For ambition, or revenge?
Were the powers of heaven spent just as heaven meant
In this unseen change?

We are trained to find our chance in Russia's vast expanse
Without rapture in this place
We're like a secret thread of doubts that have spread
All around the base.

What was indicated and what communicated
with these celestial signs so deep?
No one is destined to see, especially you and me –
Disobedient sheep.

LYDIA GRIGORIEVA

The Red Sea

I saw God's underwater world!
The fish, like butterflies and birds,
wandered in coral gardens. An Angel-fish
revealed its glorious plumage. I could not believe
this could happen to me while I'm alive,
and after death I will not deserve
to see with my own eyes – so directly – paradise...
Heaven's light streamed through the depths of the water.
A drifting plastic bag
caught on a reef - and hanging down,
glowed like a neon fish:
a pilgrim of eternity – an imperishable wretch!

A crowd of beautiful fish flowed
beneath the coral's vaults and crowns,
streamed and flowed from garden to garden,
and multiplied and thickened.
In the sea worlds,
in underwater heavenly groves of paradise
was I swimming – or was I burning in delirium?

"Today there are many Angels in the garden..."
20-30 March 1997
Sinai-London

Hexameter

To tell me how you knead life on and on,
How you turn the grindstone, bowed by endless woes:
Use hexameter, like a trunk (a heavy one),
Like the moaning wind, or bagpipes' wailing blows.

7.03.97

Waiting Hall

After a life in the thrall of this call,
it simply means nothing to me
poems for the doctor's waiting hall
poems for Casualty.

How can you live in reproachful grief,
without robbing the words of their meaning
or knocking off lines like some petty thief
- feverish, morbid and demeaning?

And so life, hallmarked by display
and noisy self-proclamation,
plays to the crowd and loses its way
in deeply dense incantation.

As if all true words, driven by pride
try to become quite invisible
while only those that verbally hide
are revered and thought to be readable.

But are the dreams for the poetry pages
really so shallow and empty
if they're for the hall were you wait for ages
or hospital casualty?

26.11.05

Sleep in the Sinai Desert
R.B.

Sleep.
With the blanket of the Sinai desert and with the sky,
that shoots up over your head –
I will cover you.

Sleep.
The starry path of pale geese[24]
has risen over you –
you're tired.

Sleep.
The wind has sifted the thick and spicy couscous of stars
over us –
by Moses's mount.

Sleep.
Head to the east, where the Bedouin fires burn –
you go on.

Sleep.
Because the English night is for a reason white and foggy,
like heavenly manna

---

[24] The ancient southern Russian and Turkic name for the Milky Way was the path of the pale birds, the gray geese – specifically migrating birds – a symbol of the path of dead souls.

LYDIA GRIGORIEVA

Sleep.
there, where heavy sleep curbed you with
                              an ornate iron bridle –
you're tired.

Sleep.
In the desert, spread-eagled from sea to sea l
ike a glove under the belt –
the switched-on metropolis.

Sleep.
My chosen one.
Sleep, interstellar wanderer and pilgrim.
May your soul wake up at the dawn
in the monastery's mosque.[25]

March – October 1997
Sinai-London

---

25   The 6th century St Catherine's Monastery in Sinai (officially known as Sacred Monastery of the God-Trodden Mount Sinai) is one of the world's oldest Christian monasteries. This orthodox monastery was built at the spot where Moses is thought to have seen the burning bush – and a bush in the grounds is said to be the very bush. The site is sacred to Christians, Jews and Muslims, and since the 10th century has also contained mosque, which the poem refers to.

Sinai

If a cat can survive in a desert's emptiness,
then a hope can be squeezed from purest nothingness,
from the barest soil. Take
a light from out of the darkness,
bake the Lord's sweet cake
from a stone's hardness.

15.03.97
Sinai

In the Scriabin Museum[26]

At the concert of the pianist Paul Barns

That first nocturne pushed up to the ceiling
but the pianist,
pulled by an astral entity,
drew a sound clear as
a glass of spring water
from the chestnut grand.

Then he slashed the sound in two
like a Sufi –
with a honed and decisive
shift of the soul.

The glassy water flowed
along the floors,
along the streets, fields
and bare nerves.

---

26   The museum in the small house where the great Russian composer Alexander Scriabin (1872-1915) lived the last three years of his life in the Arbat district of Moscow.

Ye it seemed that from the sky's height
clouds burst
and watered souls,
and then evaporated –
not the sound, not the music,
but the pain threshold
of the whole essence of being:
nature's water cycle...

12.05.97
Moscow

Gare de Lyon

A visit to the Marquis De Sade[27]
(By the Bastille) on whose bones rise
The sycamores that stand on guard
And now assault our eyes.

In the vivid lilac[28] of the nearby station,
Where time races on by stages,
His shadow escapes my rumination
Between a leathery old book's pages.

And someone else's messy fate
Brewed in the shadows for a while –
A grimalkin, part of history's freight,
Was curled up sleeping on the tiles.

The crowd's now joined in equal rights:
Beggar and nouveau riche it seems.
The space between the Paris lights
Has faded like leather on the seams.

---

27   The notorious aristocrat, revolutionary, writer and sexual libertine the Marquis de Sade (1740-1814) who spent ten years in the Bastille, where he wrote many of his works. He was buried in the grounds of his house at Malmaison near Épernon.

28   The Gare de Lyon is floodlit at night in brilliant violet.

And the words in the fraying binding
Now seem clear and hard to me.
The Red Mill of night slowly grinding,
Grinding its stones round endlessly.

9-17 October
Cassis-Paris-London

Waterloo Bridge

Like a train, Le Pont Mirabeau[29] long ago
went downhill. Or was it the Stone Bridge[30]?

Waterloo Bridge flows over the Thames to the Southbank
in a mighty fossilized torrent.
Cars run along its limey vein
like red and white blood cells.
There is no stopping such fantasy…
Le Pont Mirabeau and Stone Bridge in Moscow,
stand up on their toes jealously
and are all eyes. On the continent,
they have no equal in literary glory…
But here over the copper Thames,
stubbornly pressing against its banks,
the bridge glares, like a running line,
renowned and hard-faced as a cliff –
seething, indistinguishable from a mountain,
it flows over Thames –
and runs into centuries.

And under the bridge – a sombre juggernaut –
the water swells like Wellington's arch.

31.12.96
London

---

29   Le Pont Mirabeau is the subject of a famous poem by Guillaume Apollinaire.

30   The Bolshoy Kamenny or Greater Stone Bridge in Moscow, which is now in its third version.

A Fright

How do you get to know directly
With the grace of true insight?
While you might experience it possibly,
You can't imagine a genuine fright.

And how do you ever see for real
The unseen eventuality?
You cannot know how death will feel
Until you meet your own fatality.

3.03.97

The white air of the Vatican

I remember the white air of the Vatican
and the brown air of Rome,
the dark-gold Venetian dusk
and the suicidal blue lagoon.
The word – Bologna[31] – murmurs
chatterer, duenna...
Padua droops like the shroud of Christ.
The colourful flora of Florentine cathedrals
flakes and triples...
I remember how in Rome we drank wine
on the open veranda,
protecting ourselves from the falling star
on the eve of the fall of the USSR,
next to the villa of the unfortunate Duce

30.12.96

---

31 In Russian these two words sound similar to Bologna.

* * *

I cannot really say that I feel so lonely
While God's eye's above, always watching over me

How can people weep, feel bereft and ring their hands
While the sweet rains fall and saturate the lands?

3.05.97

* * *

When these lines no longer move within my soul,
It seems the earth has passed on; I'm no longer whole.
My existence ceases, my soul's breath's stopped already,
And so why would I speak, if no-one can hear me?

December 1996
London

* * *

What do the two of us need?
What is our reason to live?
Through the window, we see Rome
But also the Eternal city.

The smoke of fogs...
The imperishable legend...
Lying on seven hills...
Stretched through the universe.

5.12.96

* * *

Here I am! Now you have me,
With my insomniac tendency
And my baggage,
All weighed down with a great sadness
But with a dashing edge of madness.
Will we manage?

Here I am! As large as life, yes.
With many dreams begrimed, I guess,
With dust and ashes,
With all my worries and my doubts,
With my fate, that ends in fall-outs
And with clashes.

Here I am! With my food fads still.
Did I come by my free will?
More or less –
Where omul[32] turn out to be vobla[33]
Where happiness turns to a cobra.
Oh yes... Oh yes...

17.06.05

---

32   A prized fish caught in Lake Baikal.

33   Common caspian roach often salted, and popular with beer in Russia.

* * *

It hurts them to stand in dazzling rays -
Those black angels in the winter beds
The translucent veil of mourning days
Blackest lace and blackest threads.

When I wake, or go to bed, I see
The mourning angel with its burned wing blight
Exposed in the garden pitilessly
To the fierce and scorching light.

21.11.05

City on the Camel Rug

I want to know just where she goes
For who, for what and why.
This staircase leads to... no-one knows...
Maybe just up to the sky.

This street is clearly a cul de sac
But she dives down under the sheet
What did she dream that she'd bring back?
Who did she hope to meet?

What is this house? I want to be told.
Where do I hide from the heat?
I, a strange traveller – from a city as old
As the Bible, with empty streets.

Who was it that piled up this city mound
Struck by hunger, plague and hail?
In many a dictionary, 'wanderer' is found
Next to 'trouble'[34], I think, without fail.

Her shadow fell on the hot, white stone
What forced her to bend her back?
Surely she cannot dream on her own
To leave and never come back?

And if the sandy old walls crowd in
She must run to the desert outside.
I wish I could see her eyes and look in -
Are they really so empty and wide?

---

34   In Russian, 'bedouin' and 'beda' are adjacent in the dictionary.

Stone and sand, terracotta and dun,
A scorched mirage on the edge of the cliff
Why does it seem home to no-one
As if after an explosion... as if...

I'd like to know why this camel mat
Handwoven by Tarik the night wanderer
Has stretched itself out far beyond flat
Into imaginery space and the future.

LYDIA GRIGORIEVA

Evening Cats

As the vacant blue dusk gently trembles
With germs of gold light faintly glimmering,
The evening cats start to assemble.
They flow into my garden, quietly shimmering.

Here not a whisper is known
And silence explodes with a crackling
And silver seeds softly are blown,
And flow over the lawn like salmon spawning.

The fluffy tails are curled over.
The inaudible evening cats pass
Flowing without touching the clover,
Sowing stars deep in the grass.

They drop on the thick, soggy soil -
These priceless heavenly caches.
In night gardens when worlds start to boil:
Thunder rolls, lightning flashes.

31 July 1999
London

The Starry Garden

To care for a garden well, you need to read the stars too.
So gardeners don't sleep at night. They get into a stew
Worrying about all their personal querks
                                   and messy emotions, you know...
And it seems like flowers float free from gravity and
hover like some UFOs.

To write your poetry well,
                         be a heron in the universe's water:
Dipping one leg into green
                         starry depths with never a totter.
Standing still, never moving, gazing at
                         the golden glow of endless worlds
While flowers and birds floats by, twinkling,
                               spinning and unfurled.

Even for an adept, you see, it is easy
                         to become lost in this cosmos:
As you go further, the more stars, flowers
                         and birds merge and you're at a loss.
How can a gardener count this infinity,
                         if so confused by their rich affinity?
It seems genius and gardening lie –
                         or stand or walk – in close proximity.

Especially in August, remember this:
                         the garden grows and flies en masse
And the obsessive gardener finds his place,
                         with his rather strange spyglass.

LYDIA GRIGORIEVA

Both sonneteer and gardener – I must admit,
                              I really like this idle pair –
Count stars, hanging upside down
                              from earth's globe, in mid-air.

24 August 1998
London

Smoke of the Fatherland

It's five after noon, and I'm not alive;
Time is running out quickly.
Through waist high grass, then, I will drive
The old lawnmower, slowly.

Is Tilford's old bridge over the Wey[35]
To blame for this deep melancholy?
The nightingale's song seems empty today
In this lovely, alien territory.

I anger God – why I can't tell –
With the meaningless thoughts that I vent.
In this beautiful land, jasmine won't smell;
Even lilacs, it seems, have no scent.

The night is approaching, The dusk's in the sky.
Glimmers of old hopes are vanished.
Has that vain time forever gone by?
Is that bloody era now banished?

Of my Fatherland, lost in thick smoke,
I will weep for a while:
In the cut grass, beneath the old oak,
With an English pub over the stile...

July 1992, *Tilford Bridge* –
10 January 1997, *London*

---

[35] Tilford Bridge is a historic stone bridge over the River Wey at Tilford Green near Farnham in Surrey, built by the Monks of nearby Waverley Abbey in the 13th century.

"From above, Paris looks like our aul[36] *from Charmoi-lam mountain..."*
Sultan Yashurkaev [37]

You can see Europe from here.
You rather like it, I see.
So here's to Brussels, my dear!
And here's to gay Paris!

You've come far across the tide
In the footsteps of Peter the Great[38]
To fling Europe's window wide –
It's not been washed of late.

Admit you're feeling tired and drained:
You can no longer run away.
And now they have let you remain –
Just pay!

11.04.03
London - Brussels

---

36   Chechen village.

37   Chechen writer.

38   In 1697, the young Peter the Great travelled incognito to Europe to learn about the latest developments, especially in shipbuilding, reaching Holland in 1697, and London in 1698. In London, he stayed in the house of famous diarist John Evelyn in Deptford, where he worked in the dockyard. I have written a play about it, entitled 'Numismata'.

* * *

A respectable idea entered

My head this morning.
She left her personal car
by the gate
and introduced herself:
"I am an idea. All great people
have had me at nights.
Now I condescend to you –
Since you're so young and reserved."

And she put her bare, hairy legs
on my desk.

I looked closer:
red, sensual mouth,
immaculate tuxedo
and bare, masculine legs…

"Are you sure…?" I began saying.
"Fool!" The Idea turned abruptly
and strode out of my head.

Now I sleep long in the mornings
and diligently close my eyes,
and listen for the rustle under my window
of the personal cars of the Great Ideas.

7.01.67
Kazan

LYDIA GRIGORIEVA

Weeping for the Empire

Memories rise up again and again
So I won't waste time's richness in vain.
I was raised in the vast, open terrane
And I will cry out in pain!

Out in the steppes where dry winds blow
I was born under a falling star.
I've made it through life and now I can show
My medals and a bravery bar…

Rifling through tokens of times of old
I see the gains and losses that hit us.
The promises made and the lies that were told,
The bans and rules laid upon us.

As if running between torrents of rain,
I hear the ignorance and the profanity,
The idols and tyrants come back again,
Clattering loudly around me.

Though forced out by storm and a false friend,
I never slipped up on the steep scree.
I grew up in the snow at the world's end
In Polar extremity.

I wandered aimlessly from day to day
Through quarrels, and the weeding of fate.
But no 'new foundations' could lead me astray
Or had power to intoxicate.

We laughed at ourselves. We mocked in our hearts.
And reduced ourselves to a shadow.
Then the country was sharply divided in parts
 Like a knife slash right through its torso.

I'm scrolling idly through the past
But it's all gone now, far beyond mending.
Yet I see that one-sixth shard on the map at the last
And I find myself yearning and crying.

2.
The dome of heaven arched over me – blue,
Blue like a giant nylon sheet.
But I love the sharp North, and its space too --
Its sparseness, distance and weight.

Where bitter resin oozes from pines,
And even the wind will freeze
And my young father's alive and fine –
And I'm in love with the Arctic seas.

If memory can temper this animal drive
I'll forget what occurred long ago –
Unbewitch myself, and gradually strive
To love what I see through the window.

3.
A high price is paid
A time of uneasiness
As the world has betrayed
An empire of kindness.

LYDIA GRIGORIEVA

Shouting on quays
Loading up carelessly –
Armenian griefs,
Uzbek silks hastily.

Hammering like beasts
Their aspen stakes
Into Georgian feasts,
Into St John's wort flakes.

The risks were neglected
And infection arose:
Errors uncorrected
And naked zeros.

Russian soil like toast –
A splintering waste
Moldovan roast –
Such a bitter taste.

Though a small thing
To kick up a fuss over,
It's hard to stop longing
For Ukrainian butter.

Each went to his dwelling,
His very own pole,
But his everyday drinking's
Not the Balsam[39] of old…

---

39   Riga Black Balsam is a Latvian herbal liqueur made from 24

The Palace of Winds

Your caresses covered me
In between my dreams.
The silk sheets spread over me,
With their bird and elephant themes,

Had no weight. And yet
They pressed softly from above
Upon my body: the silk net
Of this bond of love.

Now tell me, will you, please
Where would it look finer?
On a Raja at his ease
Or the Maharajah?

Where the filigree lily
Threaded through with gold
Yields to bougainvillea
In pink Jaipur, so old.

Worn parapets of stone.
A milky marble sanctuary.
Rough winds softly moan
Amid pink palatial rosary.

---

herbs and plant oils in strong vodka It has a bitter taste, but with an underlying sweetness, and is said to be a great cold cure. The Russian empresss Catherine the Great was supposed to have been cured of a sickness by Riga Black on a visit to Latvia.

LYDIA GRIGORIEVA

Love fills the darkness of the night
Passions sharp as scissor blades.
Cracked mirrors scatter light
In the chambers of the sultry maids.

The hot rustling of wingbeats
In the unfamiliar dusky city,
Beneath the silken sheets
Which you laid gently over me.

The pale moon's silver overlays
A glittering frosty veil
As the Palace of Winds displays
Its vivid peacock's tail.

2005
India, Jaipur

* * *

Well, my friend,
We are trapped together in a tin.
Metallic rustling marks the minutes
Of this impenetrable veil of rain,
As we stay locked
Accidentally – on the inside.

And maybe it's not rain that raps the roof,
Just us, unable to restrain the tears...
Yes, we could've been warm if we'd got into one bed –
Wrapping ourselves with one blanket.

Who makes a profit?
Where is the robust interest on capital
For the fact that two people are locked
To the very depths of their souls?..
Who has made it up? Who was so clever?

September 1970
Moscow

A Dream

A tram running by on long legs,
people drawing funny faces on
steamy windows.
A man whose clothes (with no skin beneath,
Just nerves – blue as the cold)
look like a bad translation from Russian,
struggling to understand who he is.
And then, from a yellow house
(maybe an institute of economy and finance)
                             someone else's secrets emerge
with big eyes
and a shaggy child's head.
Cats beat the kettledrums
and softly meow of innocent love.
The perverse shapes of an electric guitar
hint that it is a bastard lowlife
and doesn't believe in good relations between the sexes.
(and the guitar screams, tossing and
                             tearing – almost in two –
as if hit on the crown –
and some secrets with shadows under their eyes
look attentively into a big shiny washbowl).
And at the corner, where everyday
                             I walk to the university,
I'm told I am going the wrong way,
that what I'm looking for doesn't exist
                             and has never existed,
(and so with everything else).
A green tipper truck, looking like a dachshund,
is reading the poems of an unknown poet.
I feed the dachshund-tipper porridge

(it's my dream, I can do what I want),
left over from breakfast.
And resolve to sell
all my sexual secrets
to the old eunuchs tomorrow
(I frequently meet them at the corner,
where I walk to the university).

And the secrets with big eyes,
which stare from the pink face,
I'll keep to myself.
They are not so interesting
but it's calmer with them.
A dead stranger
approaches me in the crowd by the shop
and says that he loves me to death.
He must've taken me for someone else.

The tram on long legs
is coming from the other way.
I understand that it's time to wake up
and get scared.

 The dachshund-tipper goes on
                                    and on reading the poems.
He is trying to convince me that there was such a poet,
and he lived there, where there's nothing,
and he lived there, where I am going to.
Going slowly,
missing a beat,
starting on the wrong foot,

LYDIA GRIGORIEVA

bumping into sharp objects and shoulders,
and into the mountains of longing and unbelief,
I can't see yet where
(it's generally hard to see in a dream).
The tram on long legs
runs out from the corner
very near.
The cats begin to howl in unison
with the kettledrums.
The guitar is sneering in full swing.
My dream is coming to an end.
But how did it start?

24.11.1966
Kazan

Welsh Carols

To William Brown[40] – the painter

*"A grey wolf will come
And will bite your side..."
Russian lullaby*

A pink bear
is a white polar bear
in the sunset

a transparent and ghostly
guest

the bear's heart
is a radiant colourful lollypop
as if shimmering through
glass

green wolves
with orange withers
a child's dream
at the dawn

a lullaby
compressed in the fist

---

40   William Brown (1953-2008) was a Canadian artist who found inspiration in the myths and stories of the Welsh valleys and painted in a very naïve, childlike style.

the night corals of Wales –
a man turns
into a horse

where did it all come from?

On New Year's Eve
the Moon's axis
turns
and creaks barely audibly

a wolf with a she-wolf
make their way towards the warmth
separately

and a man with a she-man
can be seen through the window
and if together
then isn't it an elk?

elk... elk...

13 January 1999

Freud in London[41]

In his old age in London, Freud lived amid flowers
Enveloped by his daughter's tender care
As she did her sewing, he'd sit close for hours
Patiently waiting, and going nowhere.

A sitter, with nothing to do...

There are myriad small signs all around
But never a good one comes to the fore,
And the vicious, spoiled and smelly hound
Barks like a Russian patient[42] at the door.

In the dozing old man's ponderous dreaming,
The sick are coming from everywhere,
And like starving wolves they're all screaming –
Or is it Anna singing from her sewing chair?

The thin voice is so dry and aching.
She should be stopped from singing in his room...

---

41   Sigmund Freud fled the Anschluss in Austria in summer 1938, with his wife Martha and daughter Anna, then 43, and lived in 20 Maresfield Gardens, Hampstead in London until he died of cancer of the jaw aged 83, just over a year later.

42   *The Russian Patient* (1918) was Sergey Pankejeff (1886-1979), a Russian aristocrat who was one of Freud's most famous cases. Pankejeff was also known as the Wolfman, because of a recurring dream he told Freud about in which white wolves sat threateningly in a tree outside his window. Many psychologists, and even Pankejeff himself, were unconvinced by Freud's interpretation, but it captured the imagination of many artists and was the subject of an exhibition at the Freud Miuseum London in 2002 collaboration with the State Russian Museum.

LYDIA GRIGORIEVA

In confusion now, he's sharply waking,
Disturbed by the cry of a failing womb.

Inhaling flowery fumes from somewhere,
It seems he came from God's cradle sad,
And his whole life, he diagnoses, is a nightmare!
And those children... that's just too bad.

Melody

In this empty room, so bleak, so cold,
It seems a familiar melody
Was just played on a shabby old
Grand, a relic of history.

And the pianist, pushing his chair away,
Has gone outside where the flowers freeze.
His sketches and rough drafts, not put away,
Are strewn, abandoned, over the keys.

No special gloom has marred the day
But he's bowed down with thought and sadness.
Since dawn he's pondered, playing away:
Why is this tune such simple genius?

Why does someone's brief creation
Prevail upon human life this way?
What have these ineffable calculations
Of this non-computing science to say?

1969

LYDIA GRIGORIEVA

In memory of Sylvia Plath and Ted Hughes

Recall Sylvia Plath and those lines of hurt
Weaving passion and longing into a skirt
Pure linen, pure silk, soft rustling
Gone now, gone...

Threads of fate knitted in a leitmotif
Silk and whisper, linen and grief...
The fine fabric of poetic line... a silent moan
Gone now, gone...

And between the two of them, what's left?
Between worlds, between books, between warp and weft?
Sweet anger, soft sobbing, and fervid sighs
Gone, but not forgotten...

5th February 1999

* * *

The world is destroyed by a blast wave's force
The machine gun rattles away.
I rush to the house and hide indoors
But sacred scents fly after me.

It is the garden! The garden without a word
Has splashed its flowers to the door,
And spread wings over the abyss like a bird
Bearing a message once more!

For the heart not to beat with fear,
To hold on to life again strongly.
There's a vine that clings to the old wall here
Which entwines and holds it up firmly.

And the dense shady crown of the ancient tree
And the thorns of the roses around me
Provide my defence from melancholy
And the troubled world that besets me.

Fragrance flies softly in through the door
And wafts through the house with its giving
And this winged support helps me once more
To survive and to just go on living.

12.08.08

LYDIA GRIGORIEVA

The Gardens by the Palace

By Buckingham Palace, flowers bloom.
The air is filled with pollen fume
And the waxy camellias gleam.
In dense green thickets in neat beds,
They wave their chilly flowerheads
That glare like a scarlet halogen beam.

Enveloped by dense traffic noise,
The haughty edifice enjoys
The stature of an unhewn rock,
And growing from these stony seams
A palisade of earthly dreams,
A garden of vanities, densely stocked.

Behind the prisoning walls of stone
These gardens can be seen alone
If you soar above them like a bird.
And all of it you'll ever see
Is some surreal fantasy
That fills your sleep with dreams absurd.

But the living thread of history winds
Its roots in deep and slowly finds
Succour in the ashes from the fire.
So the petals froth their chilly reds
While the scent around them spreads
Through the garden – the ruins of empire.

Lydia Grigorieva: biography

Lydia Grigorieva was born by a cherry orchard in the Ukraine in 1945 but a year later was taken to the Arctic Circle, where her father was a pilot. After her father's tragic death in a plane crash on the ice, little Lydia returned to Ukraine with her mother and wrote and published her first poems there, aged 15. At the age of 20 she went off to the University of Kazan, in what is now Tatarstan, to study philology and literature.

Already, the young poet was running up against the KGB for her unique and 'unsoviet' poetic voice, aesthetically and ideologically at odds with acceptable ideas. Poems like 'Smash the window and throw yourself out...' poems with sexual secrets and abstract ideas about universal happiness, were too indulgent and bourgeois for the KGB thought police. Grigorieva's existentialism and surrealism was rightly seen as a protest against the established order.

But she always had her supporters. A well-known Soviet poet protested at attempts to shape her working, saying: "Do not make this talented girl a simple Soviet poet!"

After graduating, she moved to Moscow to be under the radar. Aware of what had happened to Joseph Brodsky, who ten years earlier in 1963 was sentenced to five years hard labour for 'parasitism', she joined the union of professional writers at the Literary Fund of the USSR. This gave her the status of a professional writer, and freed her from any suspicion of 'parasitism'.

Although much admired by fellow writers her first book of poetry was not published until 1981, after lying in the Moscow publishing house eight years. And the book had ben mutilated beyond recognition by the Soviet editor. The Censorship Committee made a lot of cuts. Nevertheless, the book was well-received and earned her a place in the Union of Writers of the USSR.

In the mid-70s, she married the poet Ravil Bukharaev. He wrote poems and prose, and plays, and could write fluently in four languages - English, Russian, Hungarian and Tatar. They had a son Vasily Bukharaev, who tragically died in Moscow in 2003, on the eve of his 30th birthday.

By this time, Lydia and Ravil were living in London, where Ravil worked for the Russian service of the BBC World Service. Remarkably, Orthodox Christian Lydia, and Muslim Ravil, lived and wrote happily under the same roof, a phenomena beautifully described in Ravil's lyrical novel memoir *Letters to Another Room*, translated into English by John Farndon with Olga Nakston. Sadly, Ravil died suddenly in January 2012. After his untimely death, Lydia decided to stay living in London where she has made her home.

It was here, in a house within a wood high on a hill above Dulwich, that Lydia has written much of her poetry, and created a beautiful garden. A Russian poet, as one Moscow paper put it, writing in London, 'in a glass house among the roses.' It was here too that she developed her own genre of poetry combined with fabulous photographs, typically either of Venice or the flowers in her garden. Nevertheless, she still travels widely, visiting places such as Paris, Liege, Georgia, Montenegro, Poland and India for recitals and seminars; And she is writing poetry more energetically than ever.

Photos

Courtesy of Lydia Grigorieva

Lydia's father Nikolai Grigoriev (1922 - 1952) in his Polikarpov PO-2 plane on the shores of the Arctic Ocean. 1950.

Lydia Grigoryeva at age five on the skin of a polar bear killed by her father on the ice as it attacked his colleagues. 1950.

Nikolai Grigoriev by his plane in the Arctic. Summer 1949.

The Grigoriev Family, Lydia
with her father Nikolai and mother Mary. 1951.

Lydia with her mother Mary at the airport in the Arctic.
Winter 1949.

Soviet polar pilot Nikolai Grigoriev, Lydia's father.
Winter 1949.

Contents

INTRODUCTION 3
A NOTE ON THE TRANSLATION 9
COMMENTARY
BY KONSTANTIN KEDROV 10
POEMS 13
    PITY BEETHOVEN 14
    A DREAM IN THE GARDEN 16
    THE POLAR DAY 17
    THE POLAC NIGHT 19
    A LIFE AMONG THE STONES I TOOK 21
    THE CRAZY GARDENER 22
    HOW WE DANCED THEN, YOU AND I 23
    VIVALDI IN VENICE 24
    CEDAR IS MY BROTHER. THE GRASS IS MY SISTER . . . 25
    WET 26
    WILL IT BE OUR CHILDREN 27
    THESE ARE DIFFICULT TIMES AT BEST 28
    IN THE GARDEN OF A COMMUNIST 29
    I'LL SUIT MY LIFE, I'LL MAKE IT TRIM 30
    I FLUNG THE DOOR WIDE 31
    WHITE HORSE 32

MY GARDEN, MY GARDEN, MY LUSH VINEYARD SCENE	33
VERDE QUE TE QUEIRO VERDE	34
SMASH THE WINDOW AND THROW YOURSELF OUT	35
SHOSTAKOVICH	36
ROSE PETALS	38
ARCTIC OCEAN	40
ARCTIC CIRCLE	42
BYRON IN VENICE	43
OH POOR ABYSS!	44
THE NEGLECTED GARDEN	46
THE AGE OF SILVER	47
KANTEMIR IN LONDON	48
ONCE MORE I HAD TO, AS LONG AGO	50
FLIGHT ANALYSIS	51
WORDS DISPLAYED UPON THE SHELF	53
MONUMENT	54
PASSION FOR COLOURS	55
I'M STEPPING THROUGH ANGUISH ONCE MORE	56
ETERNAL SUBJECTE	57
ALL'S LONG BEEN WRONG FOR ME	58
POET AND MUSE	59
DREAMING	61
THE LILAC BY THE HOME OF PASTERNAK	62
THE MAD PHOTOGRAPHER	64
I THANK YOU NOW, MY VERDANT WOOD	66
OH HOW CAN WE, CAN WE BE SO DARING?	67

AND MY GREEN DOG HAS LOST ITS MIND 68

OH GOD IN YOUR HEAVEN,
WITH PURPOSE AND WORK FILL MY HOME 69

MICHELANGELO WENT TO CARRARA 70

RAISING A GARDEN 71

AN ANGEL COMING 72

THE RED SEA 73

HEXAMETER 74

WAITING HALL 75

SLEEP IN THE SINAI DESERT 76

SINAI 78

IN THE SCRIABIN MUSEUM 79

GARE DE LYON 81

WATERLOO BRIDGE 83

A FRIGHT 84

THE WHITE AIR OF THE VATICAN 85

I CANNOT REALLY SAY THAT I FEEL SO LONELY 86

WHEN THESE LINES
NO LONGER MOVE WITHIN MY SOUL 87

WHAT DO THE TWO OF US NEED? 88

HERE I AM! NOW YOU HAVE ME 89

IT HURTS THEM TO STAND IN DAZZLING RAYS 90

CITY ON THE CAMEL RUG 91

EVENING CATS 93

THE STARRY GARDEN 94

SMOKE OF THE FATHERLAND 96

A RESPECTABLE IDEA ENTERED 98

WEEPING FOR THE EMPIRE	99
THE PALACE OF WINDS	102
WELL, MY FRIENDS	104
A DREAM	105
WELSH CAROLS	108
FREUD IN LONDON	110
MELODY	112
IN MEMORY OF SYLVIA PLATH AND TED HUGHES	113
THE WORLD IS DESTROYED BY A BLAST WAVE'S FORCE	114
THE GARDENS BY THE PALACE	115
LYDIA GRIGORIEVA: BIOGRAPHY	116
PHOTOS	119

Marina Tsvetaeva - The Essential Poetry
by Marina Tsvetaeva

Marina Tsvetaeva: The Essential Poetry includes translations by Michael M. Naydan and Slava I. Yastremski of lyric poetry from all of the great Modernist Russian poet Marina Tsvetaeva's published collections and from all periods of her life. It also includes a translation of two of Tsvetaeva's masterpieces in the genre of the long poem, "Poem of the End" and "Poem of the Mountain." The collection strives to present the best of Tsvetaeva's poetry in a single small volume and to provide a representative overview of Tsvetaeva's high art and the development of different poetic styles over the course of her creative lifetime. Also included in this volume are a guest introduction by eminent American poet Tess Gallagher, a translator's introduction and extensive endnotes.

Buy it > www.glagoslav.com

Gnedich
by Maria Rybakova

The poetic language of *Gnedich* is refined: it combines the clarity of Rybakova's syllabic verses and the sophistication of her metaphors with distinct, novelistic depictions of certain landscapes, people, and their interactions.

The novel is spectacularly designed: Rybakova's style resembles a movie projection with stop-cards at the key moments in Gnedich's life, his long conversations with his friend, and particular striking sceneries. It creates a novelistic effect on the tale about Gnedich's life, spanning over twenty years. The narrative is often interrupted by streams of consciousness and reminiscence by its main heroes. At the same time, it continues the traditions of Russian classic literature with its attention to detail and the psychology of the characters.

Buy it > www.glagoslav.com

Dear Reader,

Thank you for purchasing this book.

We at Glagoslav Publications are glad to welcome you, and hope that you find our books to be a source of knowledge and inspiration.

We want to show the beauty and depth of the Slavic region to everyone looking to expand their horizon and learn something new about different cultures, different people, and we believe that with this book we have managed to do just that.

Now that you've got to know us, we want to get to know you. We value communication with our readers and want to hear from you! We offer several options:

– Join our Book Club on Goodreads, Library Thing and Shelfari, and receive special offers and information about our giveaways;

– Share your opinion about our books on Amazon, Barnes & Noble, Waterstones and other bookstores;

– Join us on Facebook and Twitter for updates on our publications and news about our authors;

– Visit our site www.glagoslav.com to check out our Catalogue and subscribe to our Newsletter.

Glagoslav Publications is getting ready to release a new collection and planning some interesting surprises — stay with us to find out!

Glagoslav Publications
Office 36, 88-90 Hatton Garden
EC1N 8PN London, UK
Tel: + 44 (0) 20 32 86 99 82
Email: contact@glagoslav.com

Glagoslav Publications Catalogue

- *The Time of Women* by Elena Chizhova
- *Sin* by Zakhar Prilepin
- *Hardly Ever Otherwise* by Maria Matios
- *Khatyn* by Ales Adamovich
- *Christened with Crosses* by Eduard Kochergin
- *The Vital Needs of the Dead* by Igor Sakhnovsky
- *A Poet and Bin Laden* by Hamid Ismailov
- *Kobzar* by Taras Shevchenko
- *White Shanghai* by Elvira Baryakina
- *The Stone Bridge* by Alexander Terekhov
- *King Stakh's Wild Hunt* by Uladzimir Karatkevich
- *Depeche Mode* by Serhii Zhadan
- *Herstories*, An Anthology of New Ukrainian Women Prose Writers
- *The Battle of the Sexes Russian Style* by Nadezhda Ptushkina
- *A Book Without Photographs* by Sergey Shargunov
- *Sankya* by Zakhar Prilepin
- *Wolf Messing - The True Story of Russia`s Greatest Psychic* by Tatiana Lungin
- *Good Stalin* by Victor Erofeyev
- *Solar Plexus* by Rustam Ibragimbekov
- *Don't Call me a Victim!* by Dina Yafasova
- *A History of Belarus* by Lubov Bazan
- *Children's Fashion of the Russian Empire* by Alexander Vasiliev
- *Heroes of the 90s - People and Money. The Modern History of Russian Capitalism*
- *Boris Yeltsin - The Decade that Shook the World* by Boris Minaev
- *A Man Of Change - A study of the political life of Boris Yeltsin*
- *Gnedich* by Maria Rybakova
- *Marina Tsvetaeva - The Essential Poetry*
- *Multiple Personalities* by Tatyana Shcherbina
- *The Investigator* by Margarita Khemlin
- *Leo Tolstoy – Flight from paradise* by Pavel Basinsky
- *Moscow in the 1930* by Natalia Gromova
- *Alpine Ballad* by Vasil Bykau
- *The Tale of Aypi* by Ak Welsapar
- *The Complete Correspondence of Hryhory Skovoroda*

More coming soon…

www.ingramcontent.com/pod-product-compliance
Lightning Source LLC
Chambersburg PA
CBHW020910080526
44589CB00011B/525